The Good Garden

How One Family Went from Hunger to Having Enough

Written by **Katie Smith Milway**

Illustrated by **Sylvie Daigneault**

CitizenKid™

A collection of books that inform children about the
world and inspire them to be better global citizens

Kids Can Press

Hunger on the Hillside

María Luz Duarte scrapes the dry, brown earth with her hoe. Her family's corn is short and scrawny this season.

"Why do you frown, María Luz?" asks her father.

She looks up and smiles. She loves to garden with her *padre.* She has helped him burn the weeds off their land to prepare it for planting. She has poked holes in the earth and pressed corn and bean seeds into them. Soon they will pick the cobs and shuck the beans and pile their crops in the cookhouse to dry. So many of María Luz's memories have grown from this patch of earth. But now she is worried.

"Has the land lost its goodness, Papa?"

Her father lowers his head. When he looks up, there is sadness in his eyes. "I fear it may be so."

Hard Choices

María Luz and her family live in the hills of Honduras. Like the other *campesinos* who farm nearby, they have a small plot of land that, in good years, grows just enough food to feed them. But this is not a good year. Poor rains have kept the corn from growing tall, and insects have eaten holes in the stalks. Their harvest will be small, so small that they may even have to eat the seeds they should save to plant in the spring.

That night, María Luz overhears her father speaking in low tones. "Do not let the children go hungry, *madre*," her father says. "Eat the seeds if you must. I will go to the highlands to earn money for more seeds to plant in the spring."

But if Papa cannot find work, María Luz knows what will happen. He will have to borrow seeds from the grain buyer, the *coyote*, who will make the Duartes pay back three times the seeds he lends. The *coyote* makes money from poor farmers and gives them debt in return.

If their crops fail again, it will be worse. The Duartes will lose their farm to the *coyote* and have to find new land.

Helping Hands

On the day Papa is to leave, María Luz watches her baby brother, Pepito, while her mother pounds corn to make *tortilla* dough. Before he goes, her father will have his favorite meal — warm *tortillas*, fried plantains and beans topped with fresh cream.

As her father sits down to eat, María Luz hides the pot of cream behind her back. "I need something sweet," says Papa. "Here I am!" says María Luz. "Ah yes, you are sweet, *mi cariño*, but you are not so good on beans." It is an old joke between them, and it makes them both smile.

"I have something important to ask you," Papa continues. "Your mother will be busy caring for you and Pepito while I am gone. I need you to care for our land. Can you plant our winter vegetables?"

María Luz knows how important the tomatoes, chilies and onions are for extra food and to make their meals taste good. She is proud to be asked and nods.

When it is time to leave, Papa kisses Mama and Pepito. He bends down and hugs María Luz tightly. "*Hasta pronto, mi niña*," he whispers. "I will see you soon." Then, turning quickly, he walks down the path.

Opening Minds

The wind pulls at María Luz's hair as she walks to school. The dry season has set in, and there is dust in the air and wispy clouds high above. As she walks, she thinks of her father in the highlands. He has been gone for three months now. Could he be looking at the same clouds?

The village school has just one room for all eighty students. It is crowded and dark. María Luz slides onto a bench beside her *amigo*, Alfredo Gonzales.

This year the students have a surprise — a new teacher. His name, he tells them, is Don Pedro Morales. He is not much taller than María Luz, but he has big ideas.

The first week Don Pedro teaches his students how to make … windows. "This school is good for bats and owls, but not for children," he exclaims, flapping his arms. Soon there is daylight streaming into the classroom, making it easier for María Luz and the others to read and write.

After class, Don Pedro picks up a hoe and climbs up the low hill behind the school. María Luz is curious. "Are you making a garden?" she asks. Don Pedro nods. "Well, it will not grow much." She tells him of her garden, and how the land has gone bad.

Don Pedro stops his hoeing. "Then, there is only one solution, *Señorita*. We must feed the soil and make it good again."

Feeding the Soil

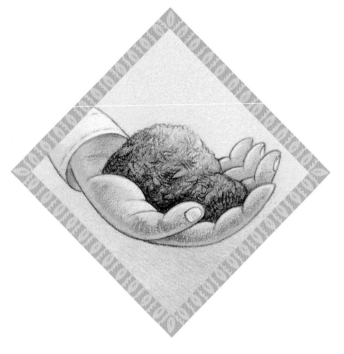

Don Pedro heaps up old leaves, corn husks and bean pods. María Luz has watched her father do the same, then burn this waste.

But Don Pedro does not burn it — he says he is making food for the soil instead. He covers the pile with a big piece of plastic. With the help of worms and grubs, he explains, the old plants will break down into food for the soil called compost.

Don Pedro asks María Luz to stir the compost every day with a stick and make sure it stays damp. He will collect manure from the school's chicken coop and add it to the pile. "Our soil will have a feast," he says.

"*Sí, sí,*" laughs Alfredo, who is passing by. "María Luz will make dirt soup!"

But María Luz just smiles. She stirs the compost and imagines Papa eating his plantains, *tortillas*, beans and cream. Can a garden have a favorite meal, too?

Shaping the Land

Don Pedro's next gardening project is a big one. María Luz watches as he shovels the soil into giant steps he calls terraces. They rise like a staircase up the hill behind the school.

Many people in town come to see the spectacle. Some of them point and shake their heads. But they listen when Don Pedro explains that the terraces make flat surfaces for planting and keep the soil from washing downhill with the rains. On the side of each step, he plants vines and grass to hold the terrace in place.

Don Pedro mixes rich compost into the soil, then pokes holes in the terraces and plants his seeds. The *campesinos* nod and whisper but fall silent when the *maestro* plants marigolds in rows beside the seeds. Has he gone *loco*, they wonder? "It may look crazy," laughs Don Pedro,

"but the marigolds will keep the insects away."

Over the next few days, more and more families come by to watch and learn. Some ask Don Pedro how to make terraces. Others ask María Luz how to make compost. Still others admire the marigolds, which Don Pedro calls the smiles of the soil. Everyone is wondering the same thing — could these new ideas help their gardens, too?

But it is too late for one family. Alfredo's parents have run out of corn, and the *coyote* will not lend them more. They must leave their land and go to live with relatives. María Luz waves sadly to Alfredo as he helps his family carry off their belongings. María Luz knows the same thing could happen to her family and to many other families in the village.

Planting the Seeds

María Luz begins to try some of Don Pedro's new ways at home. She makes small terraces for her family's winter vegetables. Her steps look rough and uneven, but they will hold the soil.

Pepito toddles out to see. He grabs a handful of compost and pats it onto a terrace, just as he has seen his big sister do. Won't Papa be surprised to find two gardeners when he comes home!

She remembers all her father has taught her. She pokes holes in the soil and pushes the seeds down deep. She saves one small terrace for something new. Don Pedro has given her a packet of radish seeds. He says they will sprout in just a few weeks and sell for a good price at the market.

María Luz pictures the coins she will earn and dreams of what she might do with them: Should she take Pepito for his vaccinations or save to buy a burro? Pepito pulls at her to go. She gives his little hand a squeeze and picks up the watering can. "We have fed our soil, Pepito. Now we must give it a drink."

The work has made them hungry, but María Luz knows that only a small mound of beans and a little *tortilla* dough remain. Once these are gone, they will have nothing. Unless her father has found work, her radish money may not go to her dreams but to buy food.

Tending Young Shoots

The air is growing warmer, and the school's little hillside is sprouting. The garden is now part of their classroom. Don Pedro asks his students to count the radish shoots and to measure the distance between onions. He has them divide seeds into equal piles.

Every day at home, María Luz checks her vegetables. The tomatoes and chilies are small and green, and the onions are still asleep underground. But her radishes poke their red tops out of the soil into the warm sun. You must grow fat, she tells them. You must!

Someone else is also watching María Luz's radishes. One day, as she weeds with Pepito, a long shadow falls across her vegetable rows. "You are growing crops for cash, I see," says the growly voice of Señor Lobo, the local *coyote*. "Perhaps you would like me to take them to market for you."

María Luz does not raise her eyes. Her hands tremble. She shakes her head but does not speak. She hears the *coyote* snort and watches his shadow retreat. She knows he will be back.

Just then Mama calls out, "Come, María Luz, Pepito! Come to the house! We have news!"

Coming Home

María Luz and Pepito scramble to the house. Mama has received word from Papa — he *did* find work and will be home soon. *"Gracias a Dios!"* exclaims María Luz and hugs Mama and Pepito.

A few days later, María Luz is working in their garden when something catches her eye. Her heart skips a beat. A familiar *sombrero* is bobbing up the path to her house. *Pa-pa! Pa-pa!* María Luz breaks into a run. *"Mi cariño,"* shouts Papa, holding out his arms. At last he has returned.

Papa bounces Pepito on his knee and, over strong, hot coffee, tells Mama and María Luz about work in the highlands. Long, backbreaking days on a coffee plantation were worth it, he says. He has earned enough for seeds and fertilizer.

María Luz wriggles in her chair. "What is it, María Luz?" asks Papa.

"I think you can save your fertilizer money for something else — come see our garden!"

Papa looks in wonder at the little terraces, the compost heap, the sprouting vegetables — and the fat radishes. "Where have you learned these things?" he asks.

María Luz takes Papa's hand and walks him down the path to the village school. Don Pedro is at work in the school garden. *"Maestro,"* calls María Luz. "I want you to meet *mi padre!"*

"Mucho gusto," says Don Pedro pumping Señor Duarte's hand. "Your daughter is my best helper."

Papa talks a while with Don Pedro. On the way home, he tells María Luz how proud he is of all she has learned, in school and in the garden. "I should go away more often," he jokes. "But since I am back, I am going to be *your* helper."

Facing Fears

María Luz is thankful for her garden, and so is her father.

As she walks to school and back, she notices that other families are improving their land. Their neighbors are building terraces and piling up compost. Little by little, Don Pedro's ideas are taking root in the hills of the village.

Señor Lobo comes by again, and he, too, sees the changes. This year the villagers will have winter vegetables to sell to him, he thinks.

The *coyote* goes from *campesino* to *campesino* to look at their onions and chilies. He names a price and, as always, his price is low. If they accept it, they will barely have enough money to buy the seeds they need.

But Don Pedro has another big idea. He says the villagers should take their vegetables to the market to sell for themselves and offers to show them how. The *campesinos* are not sure. They have always sold to the *coyote*. They are afraid to go to the market and bargain with the shopkeepers.

María Luz thinks about the coins she could earn by selling her radishes. She begs and begs her father, and finally he agrees. They will go with Don Pedro.

Going to Market

Market day dawns clear and bright, and María Luz and Papa sling their sacks of vegetables onto a neighbor's burro. María Luz pats her bunches of radishes, and then they join Don Pedro on the long walk to town. María Luz can't wait to see the market, but she can tell that Papa is nervous. He tugs his *sombrero* over his brow and is very quiet.

When they finally arrive, what sounds and colors greet them! Baskets of winter vegetables are stacked everywhere. There are farm tools and fertilizers, mules, ponies, pigs and even parrots. *Coyotes* gather near the entrance like dark spirits, persuading *campesinos* to sell to them. But the Duartes and Don Pedro urge their burro right past.

María Luz and Papa watch Don Pedro sell his vegetables to a shopkeeper for a good price. Then María Luz steps forward, holding out a bunch of round, red radishes. The shopkeeper examines the radishes and buys her entire crop.

María Luz watches the coins drop into her hand. She has received three times the money Señor Lobo offered. Her mind fills with dreams, but one thing is sure: She will buy more radish seeds. And she will buy seeds to grow other things the shopkeepers want — herbs such as cilantro, garlic and parsley.

Papa, meanwhile, is looking for seed corn and beans and making his own discovery. The seeds cost less than they do from the *coyote*, so he can buy more.

New Beginnings

It is time to prepare the land for corn and beans. María Luz and her father begin to build more terraces and feed the soil with compost. Then, in two long days, they plant their crops. And this year they do something new — they plant the beans among the corn so that the bean plants will put nutrition into the soil that corn takes out. Finally they plant their herbs and rows of radishes.

Mama and Pepito bring corn *tamales* stuffed with chilies for their midday meal. Mama also brings news — sad news. She puts her arm around María Luz and tells her that Don Pedro has been assigned to a new town in the fall. He will be leaving the village when the school year finishes in November.

María Luz cannot imagine the school and the school garden without Don Pedro. But she can see the change he has made as she looks around. All over the hillsides, compost piles and terraces are sprouting — and so are yellow marigolds.

It is not only the soil that is changing. There is something new in the air, too — a feeling of hope spreading from garden to garden.

The Maestro Moves On

The Duartes' corn grows tall and strong over the summer, and their herbs produce three crops. When it is time for Don Pedro to leave, he comes to say good-bye and stops to admire their garden. "Your corncobs are as fat as loaves!" he exclaims.

"Thanks to all you have taught us," says Señor Duarte, shaking Don Pedro's hand. "We will miss you very much."

"And I will be lucky to find another helper like your daughter," says Don Pedro.

María Luz blushes. She wants to say something important but cannot find the words. As Don Pedro leaves, she gives him a basket of radishes. "*Gracias, maestro,*" she says softly. "*Muchas gracias.*"

The Duarte family waves good-bye to Don Pedro. Will he teach his new students to make windows and grow good gardens, María Luz wonders? Just then Don Pedro turns and flaps his arms. Of course he will.

Growing Good Gardens

This year, the Duartes have plenty of corn and beans for food and enough seeds for the next planting. María Luz and her *padre* stack the cobs high in the cookhouse and pile up the beans. With cash from their herbs and radishes, Pepito can travel to get his vaccinations. Over the next two years, their garden grows green and healthy. With the money they save, María Luz and her family buy a small, sturdy burro and rebuild the walls of their home.

In this way, one girl and one family in one village go from hunger to having enough. But this is not the end of the story. In fact, it is just the beginning.

Slowly but surely, news travels about the good gardens of María Luz's village. *Campesinos* from nearby hills come to see the tall corn and new methods. They find a village of terraces and neat yards where farmers turn waste into compost and plant marigolds to keep away the insects. Like branches sprouting from a healthy vine, the new ways spread from one village to the next.

More *campesinos* grow enough food to feed their families, and more have money to build their futures — to pay for medicine and their children's schooling. Something as simple as having enough food opens a window to greater things.

Tending Our Global Garden

The Duartes are based on a real family living in the hills of Honduras. They and their neighbors are facing a problem that is common in developing countries. In these countries, 75 percent of the poor are farmers who struggle to grow enough food to feed themselves and to make extra money for needs such as health care, education and clean water.

The experts say that people who *do* have enough food for these goals are "food secure." The Duartes and their neighbors, as well as some 2 billion others around the world, including some people in your country, are not food secure. About half — mainly women and girls — often do not have enough to eat, and 18 million, mostly children, die each year from insufficient food.

When you hear about a food crisis, it means too little food to go around at prices people can afford. Sometimes the soil is poor, or the farmer does not own the land but has to rent it. Sometimes the farmer cannot get fair loans to buy land, seeds and farm tools. And sometimes wars disrupt the lives of farmers and their families. They live on the edge of disaster, and just one season of bad weather or insects can push them over that edge. Middlemen, such as the *coyotes*, make the situation worse. They make expensive loans to farmers who don't have access to banks or microfinance. (For information on microfinance, visit www.onehen.org.) All of this means that, when crops fail, families like the Duartes may be split up or forced to leave their farms. Food insecurity makes life insecure.

Don Pedro is based on the life of a real Honduran teacher named Don Elías Sanchez. He worked throughout his country and throughout his life to change things — and he did. He helped tens of thousands of families like the Duartes learn to care for their land and increase their food production. He taught them how to build terraces, make compost and use natural insect repellents, such as marigolds. He also taught them how to sow plants that put nutrients back into the soil. These methods helped poor farmers produce good crops without the need for expensive fertilizers. In addition, Don Elías taught farmers the value of cash crops, such as radishes and herbs, to provide money for medicines, schoolbooks and uniforms.

In his sixties, Don Elías founded a training farm in Honduras, with help from nonprofit World Neighbors. Other organizations, including World Vision, Save the Children, Heifer International, Catholic Relief Services and the Peace Corps, sponsored groups of *campesinos* to visit and learn new ways of farming. Today, these and other organizations work with poor farmers and their governments around the world to share their knowledge.

Don Elías passed away in 2000. He left his life's work to Honduran agronomist Milton Flores. And he left his story to inspire each of us to use our heads, hands and hearts to grow good gardens and to build food security in our communities, our countries and around the globe.

Don Elías at his training farm, 1992.

What can you do to help?

Each of us can help to improve food security in our neighborhoods and elsewhere in the world. Here are a few ideas.

• *Volunteer at a food bank or community garden.* Food banks need food donations and help stacking shelves, and community gardens often want volunteers to weed and help tend their gardens. Enter the name of your nearest town or city and the words "food bank" or "community garden" into an Internet search engine to find a place nearby to help.

• *Create a school or classroom garden.* Perhaps your school would like to start a garden classroom like Don Pedro's.

• *Grow more of your own food.* You can increase food supplies at home by starting a garden in your backyard or neighborhood.

• *Learn more by reading.* Go to www.thegoodgarden.org for a list of reading resources.

• *Organize a fundraiser at your school.* Try Heifer International's Read to Feed® at www.heifereducation.org, World Vision's 30 Hour Famine at www.30hourfamine.org or One Hen, Inc.'s lemonade stand challenge at www.onehen.org (under the "For Teachers & Librarians — fundraising" menu).

• *Write your legislator* about sending more money for agricultural development and support for land reform to countries where farmers and families like the Duartes struggle.

Real Hunger, Real Help Around the World

Agros International & Rural Development Institute (RDI): helping the poor own land

Agros purchases plots of land and sells them to poor farmers at fair prices. For example, Agros helped Guatemalans Catarina and Diego move from being landless nomads, due to warfare, to becoming founding members of a village on land Agros had purchased. Through hard work and sustainable farming, Catarina and Diego earned enough to buy their land from Agros in 2004. (See www.agros.org.)

RDI works with governments on land ownership laws for the poor. For example, Padma, a rural laborer in southern India, worked all day in the fields but did not earn enough to feed her children, who became ill. That changed when a government program encouraged by RDI gave her legal ownership of a small plot. Padma built a home, planted a vegetable garden and started a flower business, which paid for her children's food, medicine and school. (See www.rdiland.org.)

MicroEnsure: helping the poor obtain crop insurance

MicroEnsure makes crop insurance available to large numbers of poor farmers. Chikayiko Jacobo, for example, has a small farm in Malawi, Africa. A few years ago, there was a drought and so little food that Chikayiko's father died. Chikayiko heard about MicroEnsure's crop insurance program. When he insured his crops, the bank knew Chikayiko could repay a loan even if his crops failed. So Chikayiko was able to get a small loan to buy drought-resistant seeds and fertilizer. Today, he grows corn and ground nuts. "Now I can support my family and send the children to school," he says. "We will have enough food. We can get through." (See www.microensure.com.)

World Vision: helping the poor plant cash crops and go to market

World Vision is a global Christian organization that works in more than ninety developing countries. World Vision helps farmers improve their crops with better tools, training and seeds. It also encourages farmers to grow cash crops and sell them to markets directly. Verena Mukankinda is a Rwandan grandmother who has eight children who are dependent on her. Through World Vision she learned new farming techniques that helped her move the family from hunger to food security. She has even employed others on her farm. Today, Verena says, "It has been more than five years that we have always had food at home. I'm now training others, especially women, on farming techniques." (See www.wvi.org.)

Heifer International: making the most of livestock

Heifer International raises money for livestock to help people produce food, wool and fur. People can donate specific animals for families in different parts of the world. In Asia, for example, Heifer International delivers many water buffalo. The buffalo milk provides nutrition, and their dung is used for fertilizer or, when dried, as a cooking fuel. The water buffalo also pull plows so that farmers can plant and harvest much more. As one Phillipino farmer said, "If I die, my family will grieve. If my water buffalo dies, they will starve." (See www.heifer.org.)

Spanish words

amigo: friend

campesinos: poor farmers in Latin America who live on small plots of land

cariño: dear or sweet

coyote: a middleman who buys from farmers and sells to merchants at a big profit

Dios: God

Don: a title of respect for men

gracias: thanks

hasta pronto: see you soon

loco: crazy

madre: mother

maestro: teacher

mi: my

muchas: many

mucho gusto: a great pleasure

niña: little girl

padre: father

Señor: Mr.

Señorita: Miss

sí: yes

sombrero: hat

tortillas: thin, flat pancakes made out of corn flour

tamales: boiled pouches of cornmeal paste stuffed with vegetables or meat, wrapped in a corn husk

To my mother and favorite gardener, Mary Ann, on her 75th — KSM

To my two grandsons, Mateo and Santi — SD

Acknowledgments

The Good Garden took many years to harvest, drawn from the life of Honduran farmer-trainer Elías Sanchez, whose biography I authored in 1994, and then transplanted into a children's book with the help of my wonderful editor, Valerie Wyatt, illustrator Sylvie Daigneault and the Kids Can Press team. Milton Flores and Margoth Andrews, who carry on the work of Elías, thoughtfully reviewed language and illustrations for authenticity, while Jehan Velji, Stef Cohn, Sean Diamond and Lise Struthers helped to ensure the messages were global. I am deeply thankful for the late Elías and his partner Candida, who shared with me their lives and knowledge. And to the many campesino families who let me garden alongside them: I am both grateful and humbled.

Text © 2010 Katie Smith Milway
Illustrations © 2010 Sylvie Daigneault

Kids Can Press acknowledges the financial support of the Government of Ontario, through the Ontario Media Development Corporation's Ontario Book Initiative; the Ontario Arts Council; the Canada Council for the Arts; and the Government of Canada, through the BPIDP, for our publishing activity.

Published in Canada by
Kids Can Press Ltd.
29 Birch Avenue
Toronto, ON M4V 1E2

Published in the U.S. by
Kids Can Press Ltd.
2250 Military Road
Tonawanda, NY 14150

www.kidscanpress.com

The artwork in this book was rendered in colored pencil on colored paper.
The text is set in Stone Sans and Lil Milton.

Edited by Valerie Wyatt
Designed by Marie Bartholomew

This book is smyth sewn casebound.
Manufactured in Singapore, in 3/2010 by Tien Wah Press (Pte) Ltd.

CM 10 0 9 8 7 6 5 4 3 2 1

Library and Archives Canada Cataloguing in Publication

Milway, Katie Smith, 1960–
     The good garden : how one family went from hunger to
having enough / written by Katie Smith Milway ; illustrated by
Sylvie Daigneault.

(CitizenKid)
Ages 7 and up.
ISBN 978-1-55453-488-3

1. Food security—Honduras—Juvenile fiction. 2. Agriculture—
Honduras—Juvenile fiction.
I. Daigneault, Sylvie II. Title. III. Series: CitizenKid (Toronto,
Ont.)

PS8626.I48G66 2010   jC813'.6   C2009-906580-0

Kids Can Press is a *Corus*™ Entertainment company